SKINNY

Shots

MORE THAN **100** DOWN-AND-DIRTY DRINKS *for* YOUR SEXY PARTY STYLE

PAUL KNORR

CIDER MILL PRESS

BOOK PUBLISHERS

13-Digit ISBN: 9781604336740
10-Digit ISBN: 1604336749

This book may be ordered by mail from the publisher. Please include $5.95 for postage and handling. Please support your local bookseller first!

Books published by Cider Mill Press Book Publishers are available at special discounts for bulk purchases in the United States by corporations, institutions, and other organizations. For more information, please contact the publisher.

Cider Mill Press Book Publishers
"Where good books are ready for press"
PO Box 454
12 Spring Street
Kennebunkport, Maine 04046

Visit us on the Web!
www.cidermillpress.com

Cover and Interior design by
Melissa Gerber

Typography: Brandon Printed One, Eveleth Dot Light,
Festivo Letters, Helvetica, Local Market, Lulo Clean One,
Manhattan Darling, Pringleton, Sofia Pro Light,
Tahoma and Wanderlust.

All images are used under official license from Shutterstock.com

Printed in China

1 2 3 4 5 6 7 8 9 0
First Edition

TABLE OF CONTENTS

Introduction

Don't let worries about calories and sugar keep you from having a great night. The shots in this book include well-known shots made with great tasting ingredients, all under 150 calories! By adjusting the proportions and making some simple and sensible substitutions, shots and shooters can be made a little healthier.

There are two tricks to making drinks with fewer calories. The first is simple: reduce the alcohol. A 1 ½ oz. shot of vodka has nothing in it except alcohol and water yet still has 104 calories. Brands like Skinnygirl by Bethenny Frankel make reduced calorie vodka by removing some of the alcohol. Skinnygirl Bare Naked vodka, their plain, unflavored vodka brand, has 75.2 calories per 1 ½ oz. shot which is about 25% fewer calories. It's also 60 proof instead of 80 proof so it has 25% less alcohol. In a drink that calls for 2 oz. of vodka, using 1 ½ oz. instead has exactly the same effect as using the full amount of a reduced alcohol "diet" vodka. Where brands like Skinnygirl and others really make a difference is with their flavored vodkas. Most flavored vodkas contain added sugar, bumping up the calories a bit but also adding carbs to the drink. The "diet" flavored vodkas do not contain added sugar, yet still taste great.

The other trick for reducing calories in a drink is to use mixers that have fewer calories. Substituting diet cranberry juice for regular saves 105 calories per serving. Exchanging skim milk for cream saves 47 calories per tablespoon. Replacing regular soda with diet has little effect on the taste of a drink but eliminates all of the calories and all of the sugar that the soda would usually add. Substitutions like these are easy to make without affecting the flavor or color of the drinks.

Staying far away from any bottled bar mixers can reduce calories and reduce sugar as well. A packaged margarita mix contains 140 calories while the same amount of freshly squeezed lime juice has only 32 calories. Making home-made cocktail mixers is not hard to do and fresh mixers always taste better than what comes out of a bottle.

Included on the next two pages are recipes for easy to make mixers that replace two of the highest calorie items found behind the bar: Irish cream and grenadine. The Irish cream liqueur recipe tastes great and has 33% fewer calories than brand name Irish cream. The grenadine recipe has about 20% fewer calories but more importantly, it has the more robust and fresh pomegranate flavor that bottled brands lack. Both of these mixes can be kept in the refrigerator for up to a month.

To me, shots are social drinks, meant to be served to celebrate and have fun. I hope you enjoy this collection and have fun exploring the different recipes!

LOW CALORIE IRISH CREAM LIQUEUR

Many of the shots in this book call for Irish cream liqueur, a blend of Irish whiskey, chocolate, and cream that would normally be high in sugar, fat, and of course calories. Below is an alternative recipe for Irish cream that is easy to make at home and has far less fat, less sugar, and just under 33% fewer calories.

YOU WILL NEED: A clean 1 quart container that can be sealed shut. A decorative bottle would be nice but even an empty plastic milk jug would work. You will want to shake the liqueur before serving it so a container that seals tightly is essential.

1 ⅓ CUP IRISH WHISKEY
1 CUP UNSWEETENED COCONUT MILK
2 TBSP. SUGAR-FREE CHOCOLATE SYRUP
1 14 OZ. CAN FAT-FREE SWEETENED CONDENSED MILK
1 TSP. INSTANT COFFEE
1 TSP. VANILLA EXTRACT
1 TSP. ALMOND EXTRACT

MAKING THE LIQUEUR COULD NOT BE EASIER!
Throw everything in a blender and blend on high speed for 30 seconds to 1 minute. Pour it into your re-sealable container and store in the refrigerator for up to 60 days. Give it a good shake before serving.

Calories: 68 calories per oz. For comparison, Bailey's Irish Cream has 98 calories per oz.

NATURAL HOMEMADE GRENADINE

4 CUPS POM WONDERFUL 100% POMEGRANATE JUICE

2 CUPS GRANULATED SUGAR

In a medium saucepan over medium to medium-low heat, bring the pomegranate juice to a low simmer. Continue simmering the juice, stirring occasionally until the juice has reduced by half. Add the sugar and stir until the sugar has completely dissolved. Allow to cool and store in an air tight container in the refrigerator for up to a month.

Calories: Approximately 89 calories per ounce, depending on how much the juice is reduced.

Sweet AND INNOCENT

THESE SHOTS ARE TASTY AND SWEET AND FUN TO PASS AROUND.

ALABAMA SLAMMER

1 PART SOUTHERN COMFORT
1 PART AMARETTO
1 PART CRANBERRY JUICE

Combine equal parts of everything in a cocktail shaker filled with ice. Shake vigorously for 15-20 seconds and strain into shot glasses.

CALORIES: 86
CARBS: 7.0G
SUGAR: 7.0G

ASTROPOP

1 PART CHERRY VODKA
1 PART COCONUT VODKA
1 PART PEPPERMINT SCHNAPPS
1 PART DIET CRANBERRY JUICE

Combine equal parts of everything in a cocktail shaker filled with ice. Shake vigorously for 15-20 seconds and strain into shot glasses.

CALORIES: 87
CARBS: 5.1G
SUGAR: 5.1G

BANANA SPLIT

1 PART CHOCOLATE VODKA
1 PART STRAWBERRY VODKA
1 PART BANANA LIQUEUR

Combine equal parts of everything in a cocktail shaker filled with ice. Shake vigorously for 15-20 seconds and strain into shot glasses.

CALORIES: 101
CARBS: 5.5G
SUGAR: 5.5G

BEAT THE BLUES

1 PART VANILLA VODKA
1 PART BLUEBERRY VODKA
1 PART BLUE CURAÇAO

Combine equal parts of everything in a cocktail shaker filled with ice. Shake vigorously for 15-20 seconds and strain into shot glasses.

CALORIES: 96
CARBS: 5.5G
SUGAR: 5.5G

SHOT GARNISH IDEAS

RIMMING

In a shallow saucer, place 2-3 tablespoons of a dry garnish. Colored sugar, cinnamon sugar, and crushed candies such as Jolly Ranchers and Peppermints all work well. In a second shallow saucer, add 2-3 tablespoons of water.

Dip the shot glass rim in the water then dip it in the garnish.

LIMES

Limes are a popular garnish for all kinds of drinks. There are several forms of lime garnishes, including peels, wedges, wheels, and slices. For shots, the lime should be cut into wedges to sit on the rim of the glass. Imagine looking down on a lime from the top of the stem and cutting it into 8 equal slices like a pizza. First, cut the fruit in half from top (stem) to bottom. Next, cut each half in half to make quarters. Then cut each quarter in half across the peel to make eighths. Finally, cut each wedge halfway through the fruit from the center towards the peel. This will create a notch that will be used to fit the wedge onto the edge of the glass. Lime garnishes are great with shots that contain tequila.

LEMON TWISTS

Twists are thin strips of citrus peel 1-2 inches long. Using a small paring knife carefully cut along the circumference of the lemon going deep enough to see a little bit of white but not into the pith, which is bitter. If you can still see the pores of the peel in the white part, you are doing it right. If you no longer see the pores and just see white then you have gone too deep and should trim off the pith. Once the twist is cut, it should be twisted over the drink, squeezing the oils out of the peel. The twist can also be rubbed around the rim of the glass before being placed across the top of the shot glass.

CHERRIES

Some drinks need to have a cherry in them to be made properly. Two examples are the Manhattan and the Shirley Temple. A Shirley Temple served without a cherry would be called a Brooke Shields. Maraschino cherries are typically red but there is a green variety available as well. In some drinks, a green maraschino cherry will look nicer than a red one. Be careful to not add cherries to a drink where the primary flavor of the liquor is meant to be the focus; a drink that is served neat for example. Cherries should be speared with a toothpick or similar item before being added. This minimizes the contact with the garnish and is required by some health codes.

It also makes it easier to take the cherry out and eat it before or after doing the shot.

COCOA AND CINNAMON POWDERS

Adding a sprinkle of cocoa powder to the top of a creamy shot gives it a nice finished appearance. Cocoa powder can be added to shots that have any chocolate liqueur or vodka in them as well as to shots that are topped with whipped cream. Cinnamon powder can be added to shots with Fireball or other cinnamon flavors.

BLUE KAMIKAZE

1 PART BLUE CURAÇAO
1 PART VODKA
1 PART FRESH LIME JUICE

Combine equal parts of everything in a cocktail shaker filled with ice. Shake vigorously for 15–20 seconds and strain into shot glasses.

CALORIES: 71.5
CARBS: 4.0G
SUGAR: 3.0G

BUBBLE GUM

1 PART AMARETTO

1 PART 99 BANANAS BANANA SCHNAPPS

1 PART SOUTHERN COMFORT

1 PART SKIM MILK

1 PART DIET CRANBERRY JUICE

Combine equal parts of everything in a cocktail shaker filled with ice. Shake vigorously for 15-20 seconds and strain into shot glasses. Looks and tastes like bubble gum.

CALORIES: 76.5
CARBS: 6.9G
SUGAR: 6.9G

CACTUS JACK

1 PART WHISKEY
1 PART PINEAPPLE VODKA
1 PART ORANGE JUICE

Combine equal parts of everything in a cocktail shaker filled with ice. Shake vigorously for 15-20 seconds and strain into shot glasses.

CALORIES: 72
CARBS: 2.5G
SUGAR: 2.5G

CHERRY BOMB

- 1 PART CHERRY VODKA
- 1 PART RED BULL
- 1 MARASCHINO CHERRY PER SHOT

Place a cherry in each shot glass. Combine equal parts cherry vodka and Red Bull in a cocktail shaker filled with ice. Shake vigorously for 15–20 seconds and strain into shot glasses.

CALORIES: 32
CARBS: 3.6G
SUGAR: 1.9G

CHERRY SWIZZLE

2 PARTS SKINNYGIRL WHITE CHERRY VODKA
1 PART FRESH LIME JUICE
1 PART DIET 7-UP

Combine cherry vodka and lime juice in a cocktail shaker filled with ice. Shake vigorously for 15–20 seconds and strain into shot glasses, filling each glass two thirds full. Top each glass with diet 7-Up.

CALORIES: 40
CARBS: 0.4G
SUGAR: 0.4G

DRUNK JENGA

Drunk Jenga is the classic block stacking game, modified to be the perfect drinking game for any group of friends. To set up the game, you'll need a pen or marker and a box of Jenga blocks. Write different rules on at least three quarters of the tiles. Rules can vary wildly. An example of some rules might be, "take two drinks," "make someone else drink", "make a new rule" or "don't speak for the rest of the game." Be creative.

Set up the Jenga game and play as normal. Whenever a player pulls a block with a rule, they must abide by it. When the tower collapses, the person responsible for the collapse must finish their drink. Players are encouraged to add their unique rules to the game.

CHERRY TOOTSIE POP

1 PART CHOCOLATE VODKA
1 PART RED BULL
DASH GRENADINE

Combine in a cocktail shaker filled with ice. Shake vigorously for 15–20 seconds and strain into shot glasses.

CALORIES: 63.3
CARBS: 5.3G
SUGAR: 3.2G

CHOCOLATE CREAM PEACHES

1 PART CHOCOLATE VODKA
1 PART PEACH VODKA
1 PART SKIM MILK

 Combine equal parts of everything in a cocktail shaker filled with ice. Shake vigorously for 15-20 seconds and strain into shot glasses.

CALORIES: 70.5
CARBS: 3.0G
SUGAR: 3.0G

CINNAMON TOAST CRUNCH

1 PART FIREBALL CINNAMON WHISKEY
1 PART RUMCHATA

Combine equal parts of Fireball and RumChata in a cocktail shaker filled with ice. Shake vigorously for 15-20 seconds and strain into shot glasses.

CALORIES: 124
CARBS: 13.5G
SUGAR: 10.5G

COCONUT CREAM PIE

1 PART COCONUT RUM
1 PART WHIPPED CREAM VODKA
DASH FRESH LIME JUICE

Combine in a cocktail shaker filled with ice. Shake vigorously for 15-20 seconds and strain into shot glasses.

CALORIES: 78.4
CARBS: 5.0G
SUGAR: 5.0G

DEEP THROAT

1 PART COFFEE VODKA
1 PART WHIPPED CREAM VODKA
WHIPPED CREAM

Combine equal parts of coffee vodka and whipped cream vodka in a cocktail shaker filled with ice. Shake vigorously for 15-20 seconds and strain into shot glasses. Top each shot glass with whipped cream and drink without using your hands.

CALORIES: 90
CARBS: 3.0G
SUGAR: 3.0G

GINGERBREAD

1 PART RUMCHATA
1 PART DOMAINE DE CANTON GINGER LIQUEUR
1 PART VANILLA VODKA

Combine equal parts of everything in a cocktail shaker filled with ice. Shake vigorously for 15–20 seconds and strain into shot glasses.

CALORIES: 112
CARBS: 9.8G
SUGAR: 7.8G

GOLDEN NIPPLE

1 PART FIREBALL CINNAMON WHISKEY
1 PART BUTTERSCOTCH SCHNAPPS
1 PART IRISH CREAM
1-2 DROPS GRENADINE

Combine equal parts of Fireball, butterscotch schnapps, and Irish cream in a cocktail shaker filled with ice. Shake vigorously for 15–20 seconds and strain into shot glasses. Place 1-2 drops of grenadine in the center of each drink.

CALORIES: 110
CARBS: 11.9G
SUGAR: 11.3G

GRAPE CHILL

2 PARTS GRAPE VODKA
1 PART VANILLA VODKA
1 PART PINEAPPLE JUICE

Combine grape vodka, vanilla vodka, and pineapple juice in a cocktail shaker filled with ice. Shake vigorously for 15–20 seconds and strain into shot glasses.

CALORIES: 73
CARBS: 3.4G
SUGAR: 3.3G

GRAPE SOURBALL

1 PART GRAPE VODKA
1 PART CRYSTAL LIGHT LEMONADE
1 PART ORANGE JUICE

Combine equal parts of everything in a cocktail shaker filled with ice. Shake vigorously for 15-20 seconds and strain into shot glasses. These can also great on the rocks or up in a martini glass.

CALORIES: 38
CARBS: 2.5G
SUGAR: 2.5G

GUMBALL

1 PART RASPBERRY VODKA
1 PART BANANA LIQUEUR
1 PART GRAPEFRUIT JUICE

Combine equal parts of everything in a cocktail shaker filled with ice. Shake vigorously for 15–20 seconds and strain into shot glasses.

CALORIES: 73.5
CARBS: 6.0G
SUGAR: 6.0G

HEAD RUSH

1 PART PEACH VODKA
1 PART PEAR VODKA
1 PART SAMBUCA

Combine equal parts of everything in a cocktail shaker filled with ice. Shake vigorously for 15-20 seconds and strain into shot glasses.

CALORIES: 96
CARBS: 5.5G
SUGAR: 5.5G

JELLY BEAN SHOT

1 PART BLACKBERRY VODKA
1 PART DIET COLA
SPLASH SAMBUCA

Combine in a cocktail shaker filled with ice. Shake vigorously for 15–20 seconds and strain into shot glasses.

CALORIES: 57
CARBS: 3.3G
SUGAR: 3.3G

JOLLY RANCHER

1 PART APPLE VODKA
1 PART CHERRY VODKA
1 PART PEACH VODKA
1 PART DIET CRANBERRY JUICE

Combine equal parts of everything in a cocktail shaker filled with ice. Shake vigorously for 15-20 seconds and strain into shot glasses.

CALORIES: 67
CARBS: 2.2G
SUGAR: 2.2G

"I'm sorry for people who don't drink. When they wake up in the morning, that's as good as they're going to feel all day."

FRANK SINATRA

MAD SCIENTIST

1 PART BLUEBERRY VODKA
1 PART BLACKBERRY VODKA
DASH MIDORI MELON LIQUEUR
DASH IRISH CREAM

Combine equal parts of blueberry vodka and blackberry vodka in a cocktail shaker filled with ice. Shake vigorously for 15-20 seconds and strain into shot glasses, leaving a little room at the top of each glass. Top each glass off with a dash of bright green Midori followed by a dash of Irish cream.

CALORIES: 95
CARBS: 5.3G
SUGAR: 5.2G

"*I drink to make other people more interesting.*"

ERNEST HEMINGWAY

MASSIVE MOUNDS

1 PART CHOCOLATE VODKA
1 PART COCONUT VODKA

Combine in a cocktail shaker filled with ice. Shake vigorously for 15-20 seconds and strain into shot glasses.

CALORIES: 98
CARBS: 3.0G
SUGAR: 3.0G

MELON BALL

1 PART VODKA
1 PART MIDORI MELON LIQUEUR
1 PART PINEAPPLE JUICE

Combine equal parts of everything in a cocktail shaker filled with ice. Shake vigorously for 15–20 seconds and strain into shot glasses.

CALORIES: 79
CARBS: 7.0G
SUGAR: 7.0G

NASTY STEWARDESS

1 PART ORANGE VODKA
1 PART LICOR 43
1 PART DIET TONIC WATER

Combine equal parts of orange vodka and Licor 43 (also known as Cuarenta y Tres) in a cocktail shaker filled with ice. Shake vigorously for 15–20 seconds and strain into shot glasses, leaving each glass only two thirds full. Top each glass off with chilled tonic water.

CALORIES: 66
CARBS: 4.5G
SUGAR: 4.5G

OATMEAL COOKIE

2 PARTS IRISH CREAM
1 PART CINNAMON SCHNAPPS
1 PART COFFEE LIQUEUR
1 PART FRANGELICO
1 PART SKIM MILK

Combine in a cocktail shaker filled with ice. Shake vigorously for 15–20 seconds and strain into shot glasses.

CALORIES: 86
CARBS: 11.9G
SUGAR: 11.1G

P B & J

1 PART FRANGELICO
1 PART CHAMBORD

Combine in a cocktail shaker filled with ice. Shake vigorously for 15-20 seconds and strain into shot glasses.

CALORIES: 107
CARBS: 14.5G
SUGAR: 14.5G

"First you take
a drink, then the
drink takes a
drink, then the
drink takes you."

F. SCOTT FITZGERALD

PEACH SNAPPER

2 PARTS CANADIAN WHISKEY
1 PART SALTED CARAMEL VODKA
1 PART PEACH VODKA
SPLASH DIET CRANBERRY JUICE

Combine everything in a cocktail shaker filled with ice. Shake vigorously for 15–20 seconds and strain into shot glasses.

CALORIES: 77
CARBS: 1.2G
SUGAR: 1.2G

PINK LEMONADE

1 PART VODKA
1 PART LEMON JUICE
1 PART DIET CRANBERRY JUICE

Combine equal parts of everything in a cocktail shaker filled with ice. Shake vigorously for 15-20 seconds and strain into shot glasses.

CALORIES: 35
CARBS: 0.5G
SUGAR: 0.5G

PINK PETALS

1 PART SKINNYGIRL WHITE CHERRY VODKA
1 PART SKINNYGIRL COCONUT VODKA
DASH GRENADINE

Combine in a cocktail shaker filled with ice. Shake vigorously for 15-20 seconds and strain into shot glasses.

CALORIES: 81
CARBS: 1.8G
SUGAR: 1.8G

POISON APPLE

1 PART SKINNYGIRL WHITE CHERRY VODKA
1 PART NO SUGAR ADDED APPLE JUICE JUICE

Combine in a cocktail shaker filled with ice. Shake vigorously for 15-20 seconds and strain into shot glasses.

CALORIES: 47
CARBS: 2.2G
SUGAR: 2.2G

PARANOIA

The person on your right whispers you a question, the answer of which has to be somebody playing the game (e.g. "who is the hottest in this room?"). You respond out loud. If someone wants to know what the question was, they have to drink.

PURPLE HOOTER

1 PART RASPBERRY VODKA
1 PART SKINNYGIRL NAKED VODKA
1 PART DIET 7-UP

Combine equal parts of raspberry vodka and Skinnygirl Naked vodka in a cocktail shaker filled with ice. Shake vigorously for 15-20 seconds and strain into shot glasses, leaving each glass only two thirds full. Top each glass off with chilled diet 7-Up.

CALORIES: 55
CARBS: 1.0G
SUGAR: 1.0G

SCOOBY SNACK

1 PART COCONUT RUM

1 PART BANANA LIQUEUR

1 PART MELON LIQUEUR

1 PART PINEAPPLE JUICE

1 PART SKIM MILK

Combine equal parts of everything in a cocktail shaker filled with ice. Shake vigorously for 15–20 seconds and strain into shot glasses.

CALORIES: 68
CARBS: 8.4G
SUGAR: 8.4G

SHOT-O-HAPPINESS

**1 PART RASPBERRY, BLACKBERRY
 OR STRAWBERRY VODKA
1 PART PINEAPPLE JUICE
1 PART FRESH LIME JUICE
SPLASH DIET 7-UP**

Combine equal parts vodka,
pineapple juice, and fresh squeezed
lime juice in a cocktail shaker filled
with ice. Shake vigorously for 15–20
seconds and strain into shot glasses,
leaving a little room at the top of
each glass. Top each glass off with a
splash of diet 7-Up.

CALORIES: 40
CARBS: 2.9G
SUGAR: 2.9G

TORM WARNING

1 PART SKINNYGIRL WHITE CHERRY VODKA
1 PART CHOCOLATE VODKA
1 PART IRISH CREAM

Combine equal parts of everything in a cocktail shaker filled with ice. Shake vigorously for 15-20 seconds and strain into shot glasses.

CALORIES: 94
CARBS: 4.7G
SUGAR: 3.9G

STRAWBERRY BLOND

1 PART CHERRY VODKA
1 PART DIET COLA
DASH SKIM MILK

Combine in a cocktail shaker filled with ice. Stir for a few seconds and strain into shot glasses.

CALORIES: 43
CARBS: 1.6G
SUGAR: 1.6G

SWEDISH FISH

1 PART DIET CRANBERRY JUICE
DASH BLACK HAUS BLACKBERRY SCHNAPPS
DASH VANILLA VODKA

Combine in a cocktail shaker filled with ice. Shake vigorously for 15-20 seconds and strain into shot glasses. * Use only a little bit (¼ ounce per shot) of the blackberry schnapps and vanilla vodka because they can overpower the shot.

CALORIES: 13
CARBS: 0.9G
SUGAR: 0.9G

"Ho! Ho! Ho! To the bottle I go
To heal my heart and drown my woe
Rain may fall, and wind may blow
And many miles be still to go
But under a tall tree will I lie
And let the clouds go sailing by"

J.R.R. TOLKIEN

TEDDY BEAR

1 PART VANILLA VODKA
1 PART ROOT BEER VODKA

Combine in a cocktail shaker filled with ice. Shake vigorously for 15-20 seconds and strain into shot glasses.

CALORIES: 90
CARBS: 3.0G
SUGAR: 3.0G

THE HURL GURL

- **1 PART MELON LIQUEUR**
- **1 PART BANANA LIQUEUR**
- **1 PART RASPBERRY LIQUEUR**
- **1 PART PEACH SCHNAPPS**
- **1 PART SOUTHERN COMFORT**
- **1 PART COCONUT RUM**
- **1 PART DIET CRANBERRY JUICE COCKTAIL**

Combine all of this mess in a cocktail shaker filled with ice. Shake vigorously for 15-20 seconds and strain into shot glasses. Because there are so many ingredients in this shot, you're going to want to make these in larger batches.

CALORIES: 86
CARBS: 8.4G
SUGAR: 8.4G

THE OH ZONE

1 PART TRIPLE SEC
1 PART LIME JUICE
1 PART BLUE CURAÇAO

Combine equal parts of everything in a cocktail shaker filled with ice. Shake vigorously for 15–20 seconds and strain into shot glasses.

CALORIES: 62
CARBS: 10.0G
SUGAR: 9.0G

VANILLA ICE CREAM

1 PART RUMCHATA
1 PART VANILLA RUM

Combine in a cocktail shaker filled with ice. Shake vigorously for 15-20 seconds and strain into shot glasses.

CALORIES: 115
CARBS: 9.5G
SUGAR: 6.5G

WET SPOT

1 PART PEACH VODKA
1 PART AMARETTO
1 PART DIET CRANBERRY JUICE
1 PART DIET 7-UP

Combine equal parts of everything except the 7-Up in a cocktail shaker filled with ice. Shake vigorously for 15-20 seconds and strain into shot glasses. Top each shot with diet 7-Up.

CALORIES: 63
CARBS: 4.9G
SUGAR: 4.9G

WHITE GUMMY BEAR

1 PART CHERRY VODKA
1 PART PEACH SCHNAPPS
1 PART PINEAPPLE JUICE
1 PART DIET 7-UP

Combine everything except the 7-Up in a cocktail shaker filled with ice. Shake vigorously for 15-20 seconds and strain into shot glasses, leaving some space in each glass. Top each shot with diet 7-Up.

CALORIES: 55
CARBS: 4.5G
SUGAR: 4.5G

WOO SHOO

1 PART PEACH SCHNAPPS
3 PARTS CRANBERRY VODKA

Combine in a cocktail shaker filled with ice. Shake vigorously for 15-20 seconds and strain into shot glasses. It's like the Woo Woo but for those who are a bit more serious about their drinking.

CALORIES: 95
CARBS: 4.9G
SUGAR: 4.9G

WOO WOO

1 PART PEACH SCHNAPPS
3 PARTS DIET CRANBERRY JUICE

Combine in a cocktail shaker filled with ice. Shake vigorously for 15-20 seconds and strain into shot glasses.

CALORIES: 27
CARBS: 2.6G
SUGAR: 2.6G

Blowing

In the WIND

HERE ARE FOUR SHOTS THAT ALL HAVE SOMETHING IN COMMON.
LET'S SEE IF YOU CAN GUESS WHAT THAT IS.

AGGRESSIVE BLOWJOB

3 PARTS DIET COLA
1 PART BACARDI 151

Fill a shot glass three quarters full with diet cola and then top the glass with Bacardi 151. Light the rum with a lighter or match. Extinguish by placing an empty pint glass over the shot. Always extinguish the flame before consuming.

CALORIES: 26
CARBS: 0.0G
SUGAR: 0.0G

BLOWJOB

1 PART IRISH CREAM
1 PART AMARETTO
WHIPPED CREAM

Combine equal parts Irish cream and amaretto in a cocktail shaker filled with ice. Shake vigorously for 15-20 seconds and strain into shot glasses. Top each shot with a bit of whipped cream. Drink without using your hands.

CALORIES: 132
CARBS: 13.8G
SUGAR: 12.7G

GERMAN BLOWJOB

1 PART IRISH CREAM
1 PART PEPPERMINT SCHNAPPS
1 PART JÄGERMEISTER

Fill a shot glass one third full with Irish cream. Place a bar spoon upside-down in the glass just barely above the Irish cream and touching the side of the glass. Slowly and carefully pour peppermint schnapps over the spoon and into the glass, making a clear layer that fills the second third of the glass. Repeat the spoon trick a final time to fill the top third with Jägermeister. As with all blowjob style shots, top the drink with a bit of whipped cream and drink it without using your hands.

CALORIES: 142
CARBS: 14.4G
SUGAR: 13.7G

UPSIDE-DOWN OATMEAL COOKIE

1 PART IRISH CREAM
1 PART GOLDSCHLÄGER

While seated, tilt your head back or rest the back of your head on the bar (so you're facing upwards). Make sure that both bottles have liquor pours on them to control the flow of spirits. Pour the ingredients into your mouth at the same time. Don't forget to swallow!

CALORIES: 128
CARBS: 13.8G
SUGAR: 12.7G

Layers.

MANY LAYERS.

JUST AS LAYERING CAN ADD A
NEW LOOK TO THE CLOTHES YOU
ALREADY HAVE, LAYERED SHOTS
HAVE AN INVITING APPEAL.

AFTER FIVE

1 PART COFFEE LIQUEUR
1 PART IRISH CREAM
1 PART PEPPERMINT SCHNAPPS

Fill a shot glass one third full with coffee liqueur. Place a bar spoon upside-down in the glass just barely above the coffee liqueur and touching the side of the glass. Slowly and carefully pour Irish cream over the spoon and into the glass, making a layer that fills the second third of the glass. Repeat the spoon trick a final time to fill the top third with peppermint schnapps.

CALORIES: 117
CARBS: 14.1G
SUGAR: 13.3G

QUARTERS

Take turns trying to bounce a quarter off the table into a shot glass. If you miss, take a drink. If you get it in, everyone else drinks. If you get three in a row you can make up a new rule.

ANGEL'S KISS

1 PART CHOCOLATE VODKA
1 PART SKIM MILK
DASH GRENADINE

Fill a shot glass half full with chocolate vodka. Place a bar spoon upside-down in the glass just barely above the vodka and touching the side of the glass. Slowly and carefully pour skim milk over the spoon and into the glass, making a layer that fills the rest of the glass. Finally, carefully pour a few drops of grenadine into the center of the milk layer.

CALORIES: 67
CARBS: 4.6G
SUGAR: 4.6G

B-52 SHOOTER

1 PART COFFEE LIQUEUR
1 PART IRISH CREAM
1 PART TRIPLE SEC

Fill a shot glass one third full with coffee liqueur. Place a bar spoon upside-down in the glass just barely above the coffee liqueur and touching the side of the glass. Slowly and carefully pour Irish cream over the spoon and into the glass, making a layer that fills the second third of the glass. Repeat the spoon trick a final time to fill the top third with triple sec.

CALORIES: 97
CARBS: 12.8G
SUGAR: 12.0G

BIG RED ERASER

1 PART FIREBALL CINNAMON WHISKEY
3 PARTS DIET CRANBERRY JUICE

Fill a small rocks glass or old-fashioned glass with ice and add a small amount (½ ounce or so) of Fireball. Slowly fill the glass with cranberry juice, trying to keep them from mixing. Place a drinking straw in the center of the drink. Drink as quickly as you can through the straw.

CALORIES: 72
CARBS: 7.3G
SUGAR: 7.3G

BLACK FOREST

1 PART CHERRY BRANDY
1 PART IRISH CREAM
1 PART COFFEE LIQUEUR

Fill a shot glass one third full with cherry brandy. Place a bar spoon upside-down in the glass just barely above the brandy and touching the side of the glass. Slowly and carefully pour Irish cream over the spoon and into the glass, making a layer that fills the second third of the glass. Repeat the spoon trick a final time to fill the top third with coffee liqueur.

CALORIES: 96
CARBS: 12.9G
SUGAR: 12.0G

DYFINGER

SPLASH CHERRY LIQUEUR
1 PART GIN
SPLASH SKIM MILK

Pour a thin layer of cherry liqueur in a shot glass. Top with gin. Finally, slowly pour a thin layer of skim milk over the gin.

CALORIES: 90
CARBS: 4.8G
SUGAR: 4.8G

MIND ERASER

1 PART VODKA
1 PART COFFEE LIQUEUR
1 PART CLUB SODA

Fill a small rocks glass or old-fashioned glass with ice and add each ingredient in order, trying to keep them from mixing. Place a drinking straw in the center of the drink. Drink as quickly as you can through the straw.

CALORIES: 117
CARBS: 11.3G
SUGAR: 11.2G

MINI GUINNESS

3 PARTS COFFEE LIQUEUR
1 PART IRISH CREAM

Fill a shot glass three quarters full with coffee liqueur. Place a bar spoon upside-down in the glass just barely above the coffee liqueur and touching the side of the glass. Slowly and carefully pour Irish cream over the spoon and into the glass, making a layer that fills the top quarter of the glass.

CALORIES: 85
CARBS: 15.5G
SUGAR: 14.8G

PINEAPPLE UPSIDE-DOWN CAKE

1 PART VANILLA VODKA
1 PART PINEAPPLE JUICE
DASH GRENADINE

Fill a shot glass halfway with chilled vanilla vodka. Gently add pineapple juice until the glass is almost full. Add a dash of grenadine to the center. The grenadine will sink to the bottom giving the shot a nice layered appearance similar to its namesake.

CALORIES: 63
CARBS: 5.3G
SUGAR: 5.3G

AINED BLUE DRESS

1 PART VODKA
1 PART BLUE CURAÇAO
2 DROPS IRISH CREAM

Fill a shot glass halfway with chilled vodka. Fill it the rest of the way with blue Curaçao. Add a few drops of Irish cream to the center.

CALORIES: 102
CARBS: 5.6G
SUGAR: 4.1G

"Always do sober what you said you'd do drunk. That will teach you to keep your mouth shut."

ERNEST HEMINGWAY

THREE LEAF CLOVER

1 PART IRISH MIST LIQUEUR
1 PART IRISH CREAM
1 PART IRISH WHISKEY

Fill a shot glass one third full with Irish Mist liqueur. Place a bar spoon upside-down in the glass just barely above the Irish Mist and touching the side of the glass. Slowly and carefully pour Irish cream over the spoon and into the glass, making a layer that fills the second third of the glass. Repeat the spoon trick a final time to fill the top third with Irish whiskey.

CALORIES: 120
CARBS: 9.2G
SUGAR: 8.4G

Down –AND–
DIRTY DRINKS

THESE ARE FOR THE GIRLS
WHO ARE READY TO PARTY!
NO WIMPY, CANDY-ASS
SHOTS HERE. THESE SHOTS
ARE A LITTLE STRONGER OR
A LITTLE DIRTIER BUT STILL
TASTE GREAT!

ABSOLUT BITCH

1 PART ABSOLUT VODKA
1 PART IRISH CREAM
1 PART COFFEE LIQUEUR
1 PART TUACA

 Combine equal parts of everything in a cocktail shaker filled with ice. Shake vigorously for 15–20 seconds and strain into shot glasses.

CALORIES: 110
CARBS: 11.1G
SUGAR: 10.5G

ALICE IN WONDERLAND

1 PART TEQUILA
1 PART GRAND MARNIER
1 PART COFFEE LIQUEUR

Combine equal parts of everything in a cocktail shaker filled with ice. Shake vigorously for 15–20 seconds and strain into shot glasses.

CALORIES: 97
CARBS: 9.2G
SUGAR: 9.1G

BALD-HEADED WOMAN

1 PART COCONUT VODKA
1 PART GRAPEFRUIT JUICE

Combine in a cocktail shaker filled with ice. Shake vigorously for 15-20 seconds and strain into shot glasses.

CALORIES: 56
CARBS: 3.7G
SUGAR: 3.7G

BAT JUICE

4 PARTS DIET CRANBERRY JUICE
1 PART BACARDI BLACK RUM

Combine four parts of cranberry juice with one part of Bacardi black rum in a cocktail shaker filled with ice. Shake vigorously for 15-20 seconds and strain into shot glasses.

THE BAT SYMBOL ON THE BOTTLES OF BACARDI RUM ARE A TRIBUTE TO THE CAVES IN CUBA WHERE THE RUM WAS AGED BEFORE THE DISTILLERY MOVED TO PUERTO RICO AFTER THE CUBAN REVOLUTION IN THE 1950S. APPARENTLY THE CAVES WERE FILLED WITH BATS!

CALORIES: 21
CARBS: 0.0G
SUGAR: 0.0G

"Drink does not drown care but waters it and makes it grow faster."

BENJAMIN FRANKLIN

BOURBON BENDER

1 PART BOURBON
1 PART AMARETTO
1 PART FRESH LIME JUICE

Combine equal parts of everything in a cocktail shaker filled with ice. Shake vigorously for 15-20 seconds and strain into shot glasses.

CALORIES: 91
CARBS: 6.0G
SUGAR: 6.0G

BLACKBERRY BLOSSOM

1 PART BLACKBERRY VODKA
1 PART IRISH CREAM
FROZEN RED SEEDLESS GRAPES FOR EACH SHOT

Place a frozen red seedless grape in each glass. Add enough blackberry flavored vodka to each glass to cover the grape. Slowly and carefully fill the rest of each glass with Irish cream trying to keep the cream from mixing with the vodka. Drink the shot, straining it through your teeth so you don't swallow the grape, then eat the grape.

CALORIES: 64
CARBS: 4.7G
SUGAR: 3.9G

BLEEDIN' HELL

1 PART VODKA
1 PART STRAWBERRY VODKA
1 PART CRYSTAL LIGHT LEMONADE
DASH GRENADINE

Combine equal parts of everything except the grenadine in a cocktail shaker filled with ice. Shake vigorously for 15-20 seconds and strain into shot glasses. Add a dash of grenadine to each shot.

CALORIES: 71
CARBS: 4.4G
SUGAR: 4.4G

CITY HOT SHOT

1 PART BLUE CURAÇAO
1 PART FIREBALL CINNAMON WHISKEY
1 PART VANILLA VODKA

Combine equal parts blue Curaçao, Fireball, and vanilla vodka in a cocktail shaker filled with ice. Shake vigorously for 15-20 seconds and strain into shot glasses.

CALORIES: 102
CARBS: 8.1G
SUGAR: 7.1G

COLD HEARTED

2 PARTS SKINNYGIRL TANGERINE VODKA
1 PART SOUTHERN COMFORT
1 PART FRESH LIME JUICE

Combine everything in a cocktail shaker filled with ice. Shake vigorously for 15-20 seconds and strain into shot glasses.

CALORIES: 64
CARBS: 1.5G
SUGAR: 1.5G

WHIPPED PEACHES

1 PART WHIPPED CREAM VODKA
1 PART PEACH VODKA
1 PART PINEAPPLE JUICE
WHIPPED CREAM

Combine equal parts of whipped cream vodka, peach vodka, and pineapple juice in a cocktail shaker filled with ice. Shake vigorously for 15-20 seconds and strain into shot glasses. Top each shot glass with whipped cream and drink without using your hands.

CALORIES: 67
CARBS: 3.5G
SUGAR: 3.5G

DANGEROUS GRANDMA

1 PART COFFEE VODKA
1 PART WHISKEY
1 PART AMARETTO
1 PART ORANGE JUICE

Combine equal parts of everything in a cocktail shaker filled with ice. Shake vigorously for 15-20 seconds and strain into shot glasses.

CALORIES: 94
CARBS: 6.0G
SUGAR: 6.0G

DEVILS' KISS

1 PART SPICED RUM
1 PART COFFEE LIQUEUR
1 PART GRAND MARNIER

Combine equal parts of everything in a cocktail shaker filled with ice. Shake vigorously for 15-20 seconds and strain into shot glasses.

CALORIES: 91
CARBS: 9.2G
SUGAR: 9.1G

DOMINATRIX

1 PART PEPPERMINT SCHNAPPS
1 PART COFFEE LIQUEUR
1 PART GRAND MARNIER

Combine equal parts of everything in a cocktail shaker filled with ice. Shake vigorously for 15-20 seconds and strain into shot glasses.

CALORIES: 119
CARBS: 13.9G
SUGAR: 13.9G

GOLDDIGGER

1 PART WHISKEY
1 PART GOLDSCHLÄGER

Combine in a cocktail shaker filled with ice. Shake vigorously for 15-20 seconds and strain into shot glasses.

CALORIES: 129
CARBS: 8.3G
SUGAR: 8.3G

IRISH NUT

1 PART FRANGELICO
1 PART IRISH WHISKEY
1 PART IRISH CREAM

Combine equal parts of everything in a cocktail shaker filled with ice. Shake vigorously for 15–20 seconds and strain into shot glasses.

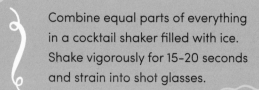

CALORIES: 104
CARBS: 9.9G
SUGAR: 9.1G

LEATHER WHIP

- **1 PART WHISKEY**
- **1 PART TEQUILA**
- **1 PART PEACH SCHNAPPS**
- **1 PART TRIPLE SEC**

Combine equal parts of everything in a cocktail shaker filled with ice. Shake vigorously for 15–20 seconds and strain into shot glasses.

CALORIES: 106
CARBS: 5.3G
SUGAR: 5.3G

NEVER HAVE I EVER

Taking turns, ask a question in the form of "Never Have I Ever" (like "never have I ever been arrested"). Everyone who can answer "yes" drinks a shot.

LEG STRETCHER

1 PART VODKA
1 PART MIDORI MELON LIQUEUR

Combine in a cocktail shaker
filled with ice. Shake vigorously
for 15-20 seconds and strain
into shot glasses.

CALORIES: 107
CARBS: 8.2G
SUGAR: 8.2G

LEMON DROP

1 SHOT VODKA
1 LEMON WEDGE
1 PACKET OF SUGAR

Fill a shot glass with chilled vodka.
Place a lemon wedge on a napkin
on the bar next to the shot. Cover
the lemon wedge with sugar. Drink
the shot and immediately suck on
the lemon wedge.

CALORIES: 109
CARBS: 3.4G
SUGAR: 3.0G

LIQUID CRACK

- **1 PART JÄGERMEISTER**
- **1 PART PEPPERMINT SCHNAPPS**
- **1 PART 151 PROOF RUM**
- **1 PART FIREBALL CINNAMON WHISKEY**

Combine equal parts of everything in a cocktail shaker filled with ice. Shake vigorously for 15–20 seconds and strain into shot glasses.

CALORIES: 134
CARBS: 10.8G
SUGAR: 10.8G

MAIDEN'S PRAYER

1 PART GIN
1 PART LILLET BLANC
1 PART NO SUGAR ADDED APPLE JUICE

Combine equal parts of everything in a cocktail shaker filled with ice. Shake vigorously for 15-20 seconds and strain into shot glasses.

CALORIES: 53
CARBS: 1.5G
SUGAR: 1.5G

POLAR BEAR

1 PART CHOCOLATE VODKA
1 PART PEPPERMINT SCHNAPPS
SPLASH RUMCHATA

Combine equal parts chocolate vodka and peppermint schnapps and just a splash (½ ounce or to-taste) of RumChata in a cocktail shaker filled with ice. Shake vigorously for 15-20 seconds and strain into shot glasses.

CALORIES: 138
CARBS: 10.1G
SUGAR: 8.9G

RED HEAD

1 PART JÄGERMEISTER
1 PART PEACH SCHNAPPS
1 PART DIET CRANBERRY JUICE

 Combine equal parts of everything in a cocktail shaker filled with ice. Shake vigorously for 15-20 seconds and strain into shot glasses.

CALORIES: 88
CARBS: 9.5G
SUGAR: 9.5G

PARTY TIPS

THE ICE RULE

This is my own personal rule based on many years of hosting parties for large groups of friends: 1 pound of ice per person. If you're going to have 10 people, 1 ten pound bag of ice should be enough. If you are having 100 people, you will need 10 ten pound bags of ice. This is in addition to the ice you might need for filling coolers. If you have heavy drinkers as friends or if you plan to serve primarily mixed drinks or shots you will want to up the estimate to 1.5 or 2 pounds of ice per guest. Shaking a cocktail or shot goes through a lot of ice.

PICK A THEME

A theme adds structure to a party. It's not just a birthday party but a "Mafia Birthday Party" where everyone can make up their own Mafia sounding name and the drinks and food all have a Mafia theme. My personal favorite is a Mardi Gras party with Hurricanes and Sazeracs to drink, Jambalaya and Catfish to eat, and beads to pass around to all the guests. Whatever theme you choose, make sure that guests are aware of it ahead of time and that the food, decorations, and drinks all go with the theme.

MAKE SHOTS IN BATCHES

Making shots in batches saves a tremendous amount of time. Simple quart or half gallon pitchers work great. To look professional, bar or restaurant supply stores sell speed pour bottles like bars use for orange juice or cranberry juice. Mixing up a quart of a shot and keeping it in a pitcher or "speed pour" bottle makes serving them much easier. All the shots in this book are given in "parts" or proportions so scaling up to pitcher size is easy.

MAKE CHEAT SHEETS

Create a drink or shot menu for the party and keep a cheat sheet with your drink recipes near the liquor. A drink menu and cheat sheet will help you plan what liquor to buy, help your guests decide what they want to drink, and help you to remember how to make each of the drinks on your menu.

STOCK UP

Stock up on essential items so you don't run out in the middle of the festivities. Keep extra tissues and toilet paper in the bathroom where a guest can find it without having to shout across the room. Keep extra paper towels in the kitchen, by the liquor, and in various hidden spots throughout for those inevitable spills. Make sure that you have more than enough mixers, beer, and wine for your guests and that you have enough coffee when the party is winding down.

Margarita
Party
gin and tonic
Rum
Menu
Cocktails
Martini
Pina colada
Bar
Brandy
Mojito

SEX ON THE BEACH

1 PART VODKA
1 PART PEACH SCHNAPPS
1 PART ORANGE JUICE
1 PART DIET CRANBERRY JUICE

 Combine equal parts of everything in a cocktail shaker filled with ice. Shake vigorously for 15-20 seconds and strain into shot glasses.

CALORIES: 57
CARBS: 3.7G
SUGAR: 3.7G

SNAKE BITE

1 PART APPLE VODKA
1 PART LIGHT BEER
1 PART APPLE CIDER

Add equal parts of everything
to a tall shot glass.

CALORIES: 78
CARBS: 2.0G
SUGAR: 2.0G

SOUTHERN BELLE

1 PART SOUTHERN COMFORT
1 PART PEACH VODKA
1 PART CHERRY VODKA
1 PART DIET COLA

Combine equal parts of everything except the diet cola in a cocktail shaker filled with ice. Shake vigorously for 15-20 seconds and strain into shot glasses leaving some space in each glass. Top each shot with diet cola.

CALORIES: 69
CARBS: 2.6G
SUGAR: 2.6G

SOUTHERN BLUES

3 PARTS SOUTHERN COMFORT
1 PART BLACK HAUS BLACKBERRY SCHNAPPS

Combine in a cocktail shaker filled with ice. Shake vigorously for 15-20 seconds and strain into shot glasses.

CALORIES: 100
CARBS: 6.0G
SUGAR: 6.0G

SOUTHERN SEX ON THE BEACH

1 PART SOUTHERN COMFORT
1 PART PEACH SCHNAPPS
1 PART ORANGE JUICE
1 PART DIET CRANBERRY JUICE

Combine equal parts of everything in a cocktail shaker filled with ice. Shake vigorously for 15-20 seconds and strain into shot glasses.

CALORIES: 57
CARBS: 4.9G
SUGAR: 4.9G

SPITFIRE

1 PART WHISKEY
1 PART DARK RUM
1 PART CHERRY VODKA

Combine equal parts of everything in a cocktail shaker filled with ice. Shake vigorously for 15–20 seconds and strain into shot glasses.

CALORIES: 99
CARBS: 1.0G
SUGAR: 1.0G

THREE MAN

To play Three Man, you'll need a pair of dice. Players sit around a table or in a circle, each with their cup of beer or alcohol. To start, take turns rolling the dice. The first person to show a three on either one of the dice becomes the "Three Man."

Play then goes to the next person with the actions controlled by the roll of the dice:

Total of 7: The person to the right of the player takes a drink

Total of 11: The person to the left of the player takes a drink

Total of 3 or a 3 is showing: Three Man drinks

4 and a 1: Everyone must touch their nose. The last player to do so drinks.

5 and a 1: Social! Everyone drinks.

Doubles: When doubles are rolled, the player can pass the dice to another player or can split them, giving one die to two separate players. The players with the dice then roll to see how many drinks to take.

Each player continues to roll until they roll a combo not covered by the list above ("Nothing!")

When it is the Three Man's turn, he must roll a 3 or a total of 3 to get out of his Three Man position. Alternately (to be more humane to the Three Man) once every player in the circle has had a turn a new Three Man can be appointed.

Sloppy Dice rule – if either of the dice falls off the table while rolling your turn "sloppy dice: drink twice and pass the dice!"

STILETTO

1 PART GOLD TEQUILA
1 PART COFFEE VODKA
1 PART PEPPERMINT SCHNAPPS

 Combine equal parts of everything in a cocktail shaker filled with ice. Shake vigorously for 15-20 seconds and strain into shot glasses.

CALORIES: 121
CARBS: 5.7G
SUGAR: 5.7G

STUMBLE SHAG

1 PART JÄGERMEISTER
1 PART PEPPERMINT SCHNAPPS
1 PART FIREBALL CINNAMON WHISKEY

Combine equal parts of everything in a cocktail shaker filled with ice. Shake vigorously for 15-20 seconds and strain into shot glasses.

CALORIES: 144
CARBS: 14.4G
SUGAR: 14.4G

SURFER ON ACID

1 PART JÄGERMEISTER
1 PART COCONUT RUM
1 PART PINEAPPLE JUICE

Combine equal parts of everything in a cocktail shaker filled with ice. Shake vigorously for 15-20 seconds and strain into shot glasses.

CALORIES: 84.5
CARBS: 10.0G
SUGAR: 10.0G

TOE TAG

1 PART WILD TURKEY
1 PART JACK DANIEL'S

Mix in a shot glass. Just do it. Don't try to chill it with ice or anything like that.

CALORIES: 103
CARBS: 0.0G
SUGAR: 0.0G

TWISTER

1 PART VODKA
1 PART CHERRY BRANDY
1 PART OUZO

Combine equal parts of everything in a cocktail shaker filled with ice. Shake vigorously for 15–20 seconds and strain into shot glasses.

CALORIES: 107
CARBS: 8.0G
SUGAR: 5.0G

VIAGRA SHOOTER

1 PART VODKA
1 PART BLUE CURAÇAO
1 PART SKIM MILK

Combine equal parts of everything in a cocktail shaker filled with ice. Shake vigorously for 15–20 seconds and strain into shot glasses.

CALORIES: 73
CARBS: 4.5G
SUGAR: 3.5G

WASHINGTON APPLE

1 PART CROWN ROYAL
1 PART APPLE VODKA
1 PART CRANBERRY JUICE
TOP WITH DIET 7-UP

Combine everything except the 7-Up in a cocktail shaker filled with ice. Shake vigorously for 15-20 seconds and strain into shot glasses, leaving some space in each glass. Top each glass with a splash of diet 7-Up.

CALORIES: 48
CARBS: 0.7G
SUGAR: 0.8G

WINDEX

1 PART BLUE CURAÇAO
3 PARTS SKINNYGIRL NAKED VODKA

Combine in a cocktail shaker filled with ice. Shake vigorously for 15-20 seconds and strain into shot glasses.

CALORIES: 83
CARBS: 2.6G
SUGAR: 1.9G

Fire Breathing
BEASTS

THESE SHOTS ARE FOR
THE TRULY BRAVE.
SOME HAVE ACTUAL
FIRE AND SOME HAVE
THE FIRE THAT COMES
FROM TABASCO SAUCE.
EITHER WAY CONSUME
WITH CAUTION.

Always exercise caution and common sense with alcohol and open flames. Never allow a flaming shot to burn for more than a few seconds as the glass can become hot and may crack. Never try to blow out burning liquid as it will splash and continue burning. Always extinguish the flame by covering the shot with an inverted pint glass. Before consuming the shot check that the shot glass has cooled.

FIRE CRACKER

1 PART TEQUILA
1 PART FIREBALL CINNAMON WHISKEY
TABASCO SAUCE TO TASTE

Combine the tequila and Fireball in a cocktail shaker filled with ice. Shake vigorously for 15-20 seconds and strain into shot glasses. Top each shot with the desired amount of Tabasco sauce.

CALORIES: 99
CARBS: 5.1G
SUGAR: 5.1G

FLAMING DRAGON

1 PART MELON LIQUEUR
1 PART COCONUT RUM
TOP WITH BACARDI 151

Combine equal parts melon liqueur and coconut rum in a cocktail shaker filled with ice. Shake vigorously for 15-20 seconds and strain into shot glasses leaving each glass only two thirds full. Top each shot with Bacardi 151. Light the rum with a lighter or match. Extinguish by placing an empty pint glass over the shot. Always extinguish the flame before consuming.

CALORIES: 98
CARBS: 11.2G
SUGAR: 11.2G

FLAMING HEART

1 PART GOLDSCHLÄGER
1 PART FIREBALL CINNAMON WHISKEY
SPLASH BACARDI 151

Combine equal parts Goldschläger and Fireball in a cocktail shaker filled with ice. Shake vigorously for 15-20 seconds and strain into shot glasses leaving a little space in each glass. Top each glass with a splash of Bacardi 151. Light the rum with a lighter or match. Extinguish by placing an empty pint glass over the shot. Always extinguish the flame before consuming.

CALORIES: 126
CARBS: 11.0G
SUGAR: 10.9G

GOLD FURNACE

1 PART FIREBALL CINNAMON WHISKEY
1 PART GOLDSCHLÄGER
TABASCO SAUCE

Combine the Fireball and Goldschläger in a cocktail shaker filled with ice. Shake vigorously for 15-20 seconds and strain into shot glasses. Top each glass with 2 dashes of Tabasco.

CALORIES: 113
CARBS: 11.7G
SUGAR: 11.7G

HELL'S GATE

1 PART SKINNYGIRL CUCUMBER VODKA
3-4 DROPS TABASCO SAUCE
DASH WASABI PASTE

Combine everything in a cocktail shaker filled with ice. Shake vigorously for 15–20 seconds and strain into shot glasses.

CALORIES: 56
CARBS: 0.0G
SUGAR: 0.0G

PRAIRIE WILDFIRE

1 SHOT TEQUILA
TABASCO SAUCE TO TASTE

Add Tabasco Sauce to a shot of tequila. Why the hell not?

CALORIES: 97
CARBS: 0.0G
SUGAR: 0.0G

SEX IN A VOLKSWAGON

1 PART TEQUILA
1 PART FRESH LIME JUICE
1 PART DIET CRANBERRY JUICE
SPLASH BACARDI 151

Combine everything except the Bacardi 151 in a cocktail shaker filled with ice. Shake vigorously for 15-20 seconds and strain into shot glasses, leaving a little space at the top of each one. Top each shot with Bacardi 151. Light the rum with a lighter or match. Extinguish by placing an empty pint glass over the shot. Always extinguish the flame before consuming.

CALORIES: 51
CARBS: 0.4G
SUGAR: 0.4G

GLOSSARY

INGREDIENT	CALORIES PER OZ.	DESCRIPTION
151 Proof Rum	70	Rum that is higher in alcohol content that normal 80 proof rum. Also known as overproof rum. See also: Rum.
99 Bananas Banana Schnapps	72	A 99 proof banana flavored schnapps first produced in 1997 by Barton Brands. It is now produced by the Sazerac Company after their purchase of Barton in 2009.
Amaretto	107	An Italian liqueur made from apricot kernels and seeds and almond extract steeped in brandy and sweetened with sugar syrup. Amaretto is Italian for "a little bitter."
Apple Cider	9	An alcoholic drink made from fermented crushed apples.
Black Haus Blackberry Schnapps	72	A 100 proof liqueur flavored with blackberries and sweetened with added sugar.

INGREDIENT	CALORIES PER OZ.	DESCRIPTION
Blue Curaçao	72	A liqueur flavored with the dried peels of Larahas, bitter relatives of oranges, grown on the island of Curaçao. The liqueur has an orange flavor to it and is packaged with blue coloring added.
Bourbon	69	An American form of whiskey made from at least 51% corn, with the remainder being wheat or rye and malted barley. It is distilled to no more than 160 proof and aged in new charred white oak barrels for at least two years. It must be put into the barrels at no more than 125 U.S. proof; in this way it is similar to Scotch Whisky, which is also aged in charred barrels.
Butterscotch Schnapps	72	A sweet liqueur flavored with butterscotch.
Canadian Whiskey	69	A grain spirit that has been aged in charred oak barrels for a minimum of three years.
Chambord	72	A French liqueur made from small black raspberries.

INGREDIENT	CALORIES PER OZ.	DESCRIPTION
Cherry Brandy	78	A brandy that has been sweetened with added sugar and flavored with cherries. Cherry brandy is higher in alcohol and less sweet than cherry liqueur.
Cherry Liqueur	72	A sweetened liqueur flavored with cherries. Cherry liqueur is lower in alcohol and more sweet than cherry brandy.
Cinnamon Schnapps	72	A sweet liqueur flavored with cinnamon.
Coffee Liqueur	72	A sweet liqueur flavored with coffee. Popular brands include Kahlúa which is made with a vodka base and Tia Maria which is made with a rum base.
Crown Royal	69	A blended Canadian whiskey.
Domaine de Canton Ginger Liqueur	72	A ginger-flavored liqueur made in France since 2007. Its earlier formulation (called Canton) was made in China from 1992-1997.
Fireball Cinnamon Whiskey	72	A cinnamon flavored whiskey based liqueur produced by the Sazerac Company. It has a Canadian whiskey base with added sugar as well as cinnamon flavoring.

INGREDIENT	CALORIES PER OZ.	DESCRIPTION
Flavored Rum	51	A rum that has had sugar and flavorings added to it. Popular examples are coconut and vanilla rums. Flavored rums are lower in alcohol than plain rum.
Flavored Vodka	60	A vodka that has had sugar and flavorings added to it. Flavored vodkas are lower in alcohol than plain vodka.
Frangelico	71	An Italian brand of Hazelnut flavored liqueur packaged in a distinctive monk shaped bottle.
Gin	69	Gin begins as a neutral spirit. It is then redistilled with or filtered through juniper berries and botanicals such as coriander seed, cassia bark, orange peels, fennel seeds, anise, caraway, angelica root, licorice, lemon peel, almonds, cassia bark, cinnamon bark, bergamot, and cocoa. It is this secondary process that imparts to each gin its particular taste.
Goldschläger	103	A cinnamon flavored liqueur produced in Switzerland that includes flakes of real gold in the bottle.

INGREDIENT	CALORIES PER OZ.	DESCRIPTION
Grand Marnier	72	A brand of French aged orange flavored liqueur (triple sec) with a brandy base.
Grenadine	108	A sweet syrup flavoring for drinks made from pomegranate juice, containing little or no alcohol.
Irish Cream Liqueur	68	A mocha flavored whiskey and double-cream liqueur, a combination of Irish whiskey, cream, coffee, chocolate, and other flavors
Irish Mist Liqueur	103	A liqueur produced in Ireland, consisting of Irish whiskey flavored with heather honey.
Irish Whiskey	69	A grain spirit that has been made on the island of Ireland and aged in charred oak barrels.

INGREDIENT	CALORIES PER OZ.	DESCRIPTION
Jack Daniel's	69	A whiskey made in Tennessee, it is perhaps the most famous whiskey made in America. The Jack Daniel's distillery in Lynchburg, Tennessee, dates from 1875 and is the oldest registered distillery in the United States. Jack Daniel's is made according to the sour-mash process, and by the "Lincoln County Process" of filtration through sugar maple charcoal before being aged in charred American Oak casks.
Jägermeister	103	A complex, aromatic liqueur containing some 56 herbs, roots, and fruits that has been popular in Germany since its introduction in 1935. In Germany it is frequently consumed warm as an aperitif or after dinner drink. In the United States, due to some savvy marketing by the importer, it is widely popular as a chilled shooter.
Licor 43 (Cuarenta y Tres)	72	A yellow colored liqueur from Spain. It is made from fruit juices, vanilla, and other aromatic herbs and spices.

INGREDIENT	CALORIES PER OZ.	DESCRIPTION
Light Beer	9	Light beer refers to beer which is reduced in alcohol content or in calories, compared to regular beers.
Lillet Blanc	20	An aperitif wine from the Bordeaux region of France.
Melon Liqueur	79	A pale green liqueur that tastes of fresh muskmelon or cantaloupe. The most famous brand, Midori, is Japanese in origin and produced by the Suntory Company in Mexico, France, and Japan.
Ouzo	72	An anise flavored liqueur from Greece, usually served on the rocks. Ouzo can be used as a substitute for absinthe in many cases.
Peach Schnapps	72	A sweet peach flavored liqueur.
Peppermint Schnapps	72	A sweet peppermint flavored liqueur.
Raspberry Liqueur	72	A liqueur made from or flavored with raspberries. Chambord is a popular brand of raspberry liqueur.
Red Bull	5	A carbonated soft drink with additives and extra caffeine that claim to reduce mental and physical fatigue.

INGREDIENT	CALORIES PER OZ.	DESCRIPTION
Rum	69	A liquor made from fermented and distilled sugar cane juice or molasses. Rum has a very wide range of flavors from light and dry like a vodka to very dark and complex like a cognac.
RumChata	93	A creamy horchata based liqueur with added rum.
Sambuca	72	An Italian liqueur flavored with anis and elderberry. It is produced in both clear ("white Sambuca") and dark blue or purple ("black Sambuca") versions.
Skinnygirl Vodka	50	A vodka brand started by Bethenny Frankel and acquired by Beam, Inc. in 2011. The brand features a line of flavored and unflavored vodkas. The flavored vodkas do not have added sugar and have fewer calories (and less alcohol) than comparable flavored vodkas.
Southern Comfort	65	A liqueur with a neutral spirit base and peach and almond flavors.
Spiced Rum	57	The original flavored rum. Spiced rum consists of an amber rum with vanilla and cinnamon flavor added.

INGREDIENT	CALORIES PER OZ.	DESCRIPTION
Tabasco Sauce	3	A brand of hot pepper sauce made from a blend of Tabasco peppers, vinegar, and salt aged in wood casks.
Tequila	69	A type of mezcal that is made only from the blue agave plant in the region surrounding Tequila, a town in the Mexican state of Jalisco. Tequila is made in many different styles with the difference between them mostly dependent on how long the distillate has been aged before being bottled.
Triple Sec	72	A highly popular flavoring agent in many drinks, triple-sec is the best known form of curaçao, a liqueur made from the skins of the curaçao orange.
Tuaca	103	An Italian liqueur flavored with citrus and vanilla.

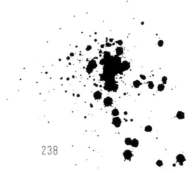

INGREDIENT	CALORIES PER OZ.	DESCRIPTION
Vodka	69	A neutral spirit that can be distilled from almost anything that will ferment (grain, potato, grapes, corn, and beets). It is distilled multiple times and filtered to remove as many of the impurities as possible. It is then diluted with water to bring the alcohol content down before being bottled. Vodka is also found in a wide variety of flavors from bison grass to watermelon.
Whiskey	69	A beverage distilled from fermented grain and aged in oak casks. The location, grain, type of oak, and length of the aging time all affect the flavor of the whisky. Whisky is spelled with an e in Ireland and the United States and without the e everywhere else. There are four major regions where whiskey is produced: Ireland, Scotland, Canada, and the US. Each has a different style that imparts a distinctive flavor.
Wild Turkey	69	A brand of Kentucky bourbon whiskey. It is available in both 80 proof and 101 proof versions.

ABOUT CIDER MILL PRESS BOOK PUBLISHERS

Good ideas ripen with time. From seed to harvest, Cider Mill Press brings fine reading, information, and entertainment together between the covers of its creatively crafted books. Our Cider Mill bears fruit twice a year, publishing a new crop of titles each spring and fall.

"Where Good Books Are Ready for Press"

Visit us on the Web at
www.cidermillpress.com
or write to us at
PO Box 454
Kennebunkport, Maine 04046